Getting Creative with

FAB LAB™

Creating With

DIGITAL
SEWING
MACHINES

KRISTINA LYN HEITKAMP

rosen publishing's
rosen central®

Published in 2017 by The Rosen Publishing Group, Inc.
29 East 21st Street, New York, NY 10010

Library of Congress Cataloging-in-Publication Data

Names: Heitkamp, Kristina Lyn, author.
Title: Creating with digital sewing machines / Kristina Lyn Heitkamp.
Description: First edition. | New York : Rosen Publishing, 2017. | Series: Getting creative with Fab Lab | Audience: Grades 5 to 8. | Includes bibliographical references and index.
Identifiers: LCCN 2016019452 | ISBN 9781499465082 (library bound)
Subjects: LCSH: Sewing machines—Technological innovations—Juvenile literature. | Machine sewing—Juvenile literature. | Makerspaces—Juvenile literature. | Technological innovations—Juvenile literature.
Classification: LCC TJ1510 .H54 2017 | DDC 646.1—dc23
LC record available at https://lccn.loc.gov/2016019452

Manufactured in China

Contents

Introduction

The sign above the door reads Fabrication Laboratory. Walking into the spacious room, you expect to see white coats and test tubes. Instead you find several computers, tables with various machines, and shelves filled with plastic spools and books. Several people, young and old, are milling around. There is a faint smell of burned wood and plastic. Sounds of focused chatter and whirring machinery fill the large space.

In one corner, a 3D printer is churning out layer 21 of 354. The hot end nozzle arm moves with a high-pitch rhythm. Opposite the printer sits a laser cutter engraving a wooden plaque. It etches out the phrase "the whole is greater than the sum of the parts." Other machines slice and dice, subtract, and add materials to various projects. But your eye catches sight of a less industrial machine pounding out a colorful design—a digital sewing machine. Like a player piano, the sewing machine seems to be designing unaided. You decide to go in for a closer look.

A kid sits at a computer workstation near the digital sewing machine. On the computer screen is an elaborate logo. He is creating personalized t-shirts for his garage band. Noticing your

Located on the University of Illinois campus, the Champaign-Urbana Community Fab Lab offers users laser engravers, 3D printers, digital sewing machines, and much more.

curious eye, he invites you to check out all the other designs that are available and tells you can even invent your own.

In Fabrication Laboratories, or Fab Labs, digital sewing machines are making magic. Based on a digital design, the sewing machine automatically sews your command. But that is just where the fun starts. Fab Labs are tech workrooms used to collaborate, explore, dream, and see an idea through to fruition. When you step inside a Fab Lab, you are connecting to a global community of thinkers, tinkerers, and trailblazers.

Chapter
ONE

INSIDE THE LAB

Fabrication Laboratories are not like a typical lab space. Gone are the microscopes and smells of cooking elements. Nor is the space like a workshop that can be loud, intimidating, and covered in wood dust. Fab Labs are high-tech play spaces that breed innovation. Similar to makerspaces, Fab Labs motivate the user to build an idea from scratch using many different types of machines. However, unlike other community create spaces, such as makerspaces and hackerspaces, Fab Labs belong to the same network of users worldwide. But what exactly is a Fab Lab? To learn about where the idea came from, we need to go back a few years.

Everything but the kitchen Sink

Back in 2005, Neil A. Gershenfeld, a physicist and professor at the Massachusetts Institute of Technology (MIT), began teaching a class called How to Make (Almost) Anything. Students learned how to turn data into things inside the classroom. It's sort of like how Spock used the replicator to cook up a meal out of thin air onboard Star Trek's starships. Gershenfeld turned science fiction into science fact by teaching students to digitally design things and build them on demand using manufacturing machines and equipment. The class was very popular. Students from across campus lined up to make personalized things—not products they could find in a store, but unique items they could not buy. One student made an alarm clock that you have to wrestle to turn off. Another student made a dress that defends the wearer's personal space. The dress raises a 3D-printed arm to flick the too-close talker away. From this popular class, Fab Labs were spawned. The labs are part of an educational outreach program with MIT's Center for Bits and Atoms.

Fab Labs have now opened up all over the world, from inner-city Boston to rural Africa. They are found in more than forty countries, with over five hundred labs worldwide. The labs all share the same common industrial-grade machines and tools with open-source software and programs. With an open-door policy, the equipment and software is accessible, so that anyone, from your grandma to your little brother can make (almost) anything in the lab. Because most labs carry the same machines, you can build a project that someone invented in a Fab Lab in Norway or Argentina.

Fab Labs have a variety of computer-controlled machines at different workstations. A 3D printer is used for building three-dimensional objects. A laser cutter can engrave or cut wood and leather. A vinyl cutter makes signs, and a milling machine creates three-dimensional molds. At the textile workstation, a digital sewing machine is used for constructing high-tech fashion and embroidery.

THINKING OUTSIDE THE BOX

What is 32 feet (9.7 meters) long and 8 feet (2.4 m) wide and can 3D-print pieces for a prosthetic while whittling a piece of wood? MIT's Mobile Fab Lab! Built in 2007, the Mobile Fab Lab is an outfitted trailer complete with the same computer-controlled fabrication machines found in stationary Fab Labs. Two graffiti artists from the South Bronx painted the trailer's shell with kids fabricating. The Mobile Fab Lab has toured the

(continued on the next page)

President Barack Obama tours the Massachusetts Institute of Technology's Mobile Fab Lab with Neil Gershenfeld during the White House Maker Faire on June 18, 2014.

(continued from the previous page)

US Midwest, the Gulf Coast, and has even made an appearance at the White House. Other mobile Fab Labs have sprouted up all over the world, including Michigan, Costa Rica, and the Netherlands.

Along with the trailer, a Fab Bike is hitting the road in search of inventors and tinkerers. An offshoot of a London Fab Lab, the Fab Bike is stocked with a 3D printer, a milling machine, a laser cutter, a sewing machine, and all the programming tools to fabricate (almost) anything. The Fab Bike is available for workshops, festivals, and educational events in the London area.

If your school or community does not have the space for large industrial machines, but you still want to make stuff, check out what it takes to make a mini Fab Lab. A mini Fab Lab explores inexpensive desktop options for the machines typically found in a Fab Lab, like a 3D printer, milling machine, and a vinyl cutter.

A digital sewing machine works just like a regular sewing machine, except it can be controlled through a computer. You will see things typical of any sewing machine: a needle, a bobbin, the square body, and a pedal foot for powering the machine. But you will also find a touch screen, several stitching options, decorative stitches, and digitized designs. Digital sewing machines have built-in computers with small display monitors. Instead of manually stationing the settings, the computer works like the machine's brain, setting the thread tension, the needle speed, and other tasks.

Another cool function of these high-tech sewing machines is their ability to create detailed embroidery designs. Through a series of sensors, the computer tells the machine's parts to move across the fabric, back and forth and side to side, to produce elaborate and intricate patterns and shapes. All the user has to do is pick a design, load the digital file, and the computer does the rest.

What Goes in Does Not Come Out

Each fabrication project begins with a concept and materials. Depending on the project idea and the machines chosen, the materials go in and come out a dream come true. Spools of a cornstarch-based plastic are used in 3D printers. Milling machines can work with a range of materials from plywood to aluminum, and vinyl cutters can make signs or stickers out of adhesive or solid vinyl.

At the textile workstation, there will be a variety of materials including conductive fabric, yarns, and threads. Conductive textiles are made with conductive fibers, such as stainless steel, copper, and silver that carry an electrical current much like wires. The materials are called many different names: electronic textiles, or e-textiles, soft tech, wearables, and smart textiles. E-textiles not only conduct electricity but they are safe, durable, and soft. Conductive thread can be used in a sewing machine or hand stitched. But the textile alone doesn't work. To make the fabric shine or blink, a power supply and connection is needed.

Some labs across the world are experimenting with recyclable or reusable materials. A Fab Lab in Mexico is shredding plastic soda bottles to produce a plastic filament that could potentially work in 3D printers. An Italian Fab Lab is digging into garbage

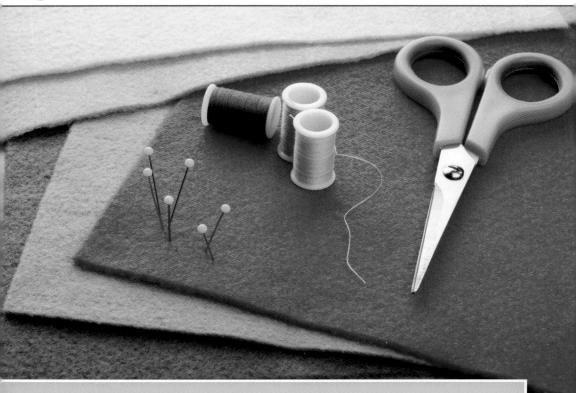

An assortment of materials and tools can be found at a Fab Lab's textile station, including colorful felt plates, conductive thread, and sewing pins.

for materials. They are recovering unused resources, like coffee grounds, and mixing it with clay to create material suitable for 3D printers. Scientists haven't discovered how to make fabric out of old fruit skins and rotten veggies, but using secondhand clothes is a great place to start with e-textiles. Better yet, go into your own closet and pull out a t-shirt or hoodie that needs an electrifying makeover.

Along with materials, the computer programs used in Fab Labs vary from workstation to workstation. At the textile station, the digital sewing machine will likely be preprogrammed with free embroidery designs to use in your projects. The software that controls the machine will vary with different models and brands. But to create an original design or logo, you will need to use a design program like Adobe Illustrator or Inkscape.

A Stitch in Time Saves Nine

Fab Labs are open creative spaces available as educational resources. In order for the space to work efficiently and effectively, common protocols are followed. They're pretty basic. The Fab Charter outlines the guidelines and answers questions like, what are your responsibilities? As a participant, you are responsible for maintaining safety and keeping the lab in shipshape

A Fab Lab's technical guru is always on deck to assist users with any questions or concerns about software, machines, or the inventory of materials.

order. Cleanliness is next to fabulousness in the Fab Lab. If you have questions about how to maintain the machines or where to keep materials, ask the technical guru. This person is usually in the lab helping users tinker and helping machines run smoothly.

The Fab Charter also stresses the importance of an open-source ethos. Software programs and machines behind a paywall or kept secret would crush the very spirit of Fab Labs. Allowing for accessible tools and software respects the lab user's freedom to explore, learn, and teach. The play space is available to anyone to make (almost) anything and to share the project with others.

Fab Labs are more than just a room filled with really cool machines and accessible software. What makes a Fab Lab special is the collaborative community you join once you cross over the threshold. Collaboration is the keystone for the fabrication ecosystem. It is a symbiotic community. Like a clownfish and sea anemones mutually respectful relationship, an art student in a Chicago lab will conspire with an engineering student in a Shanghai lab to perfect a digital file for a prosthetic hand and e-textile glove. Working together nurtures creativity and ingenuity. Remember, Rome wasn't built in a day, nor did just one person build it.

Chapter
TWO

BURSTING AT THE SEAMS WITH INNOVATION

Humans have been wearing clothing and jewelry for thousands of years. Early humans draped tanned animal skins across bare shoulders during the cold winter months. Nassarius shell beaded necklaces were worn to signify social status. Function likely preceded fashion in the early days of textiles. Today, the clothes we throw on our bodies represent individual style, mood, and sometimes social and political views. Even household pets are walking the fashion runways with diamond-studded collars and knit sweaters. Apparel design and choices are intentional and personal.

Fabrication Laboratories equip users with the machines and tools to design personal innovative fashion. Using a digital sewing machine and conductive textiles, users can produce interactive garments. High-tech apparel is no longer a futurist fantasy or something seen only on the big screen.

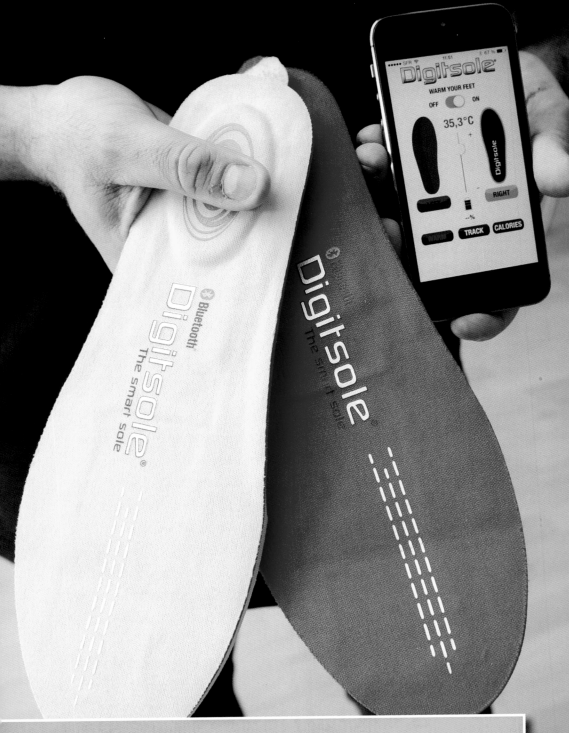

Controlled through a smartphone app, Digitsole is a connected, interactive, heated insole that allows the wearer to warm up cold feet and track distance walked and calories burned.

The Machines

Inside a Fab Lab, three different kinds of sewing machines may be available: mechanical, electronic, or digital. Each machine offers different functions. Popular sewing machine brand names are Brother, Singer, Bernina, and Janome.

A mechanical sewing machine is most commonly used in households. It has all the basics—needle, knobs, dials and about twenty built-in stitches, but the machine can't sew any fancy stitches. If your Fab Lab has a mechanical sewing machine, it will be used for essential functions such as sewing together pattern pieces, heming, or adjusting fit. The machine's functions are controlled manually and are easy to learn but finding the right settings for a project takes practice.

An electronic sewing machine has more functions than a mechanical sewing machine and offers a variety of decorative and precise stitches. It can automatically sew different types of buttonholes and do basic alphabet stitching. Some machines will even cut the thread for the user. Tension, stitch length, and speed are all controlled electronically through settings seen on an LED screen. However, an electronic machine does not embroider.

A digital or computerized sewing machine has several automatic functions. It offers an extensive selection of both utility and decorative stitches and embroidery designs that are installed on the machine or on a removable disk. The machine also has computer connectivity for importing designs to the machine. Other features include automatic threading, alerts when the thread needs to be changed or when the bobbin is empty, and a large embroidery area for creating complex designs. The digital sewing machine can sew in sixteen different

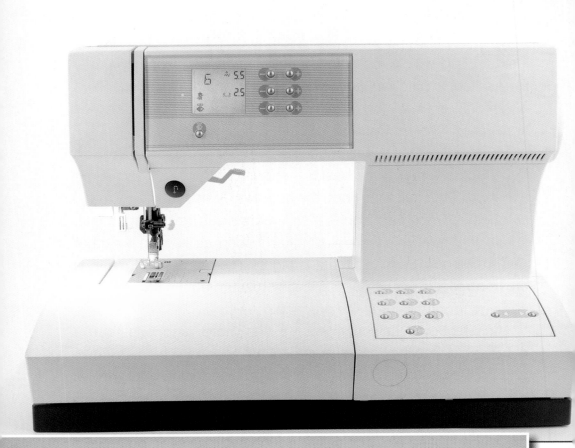

directions, shifting and moving the fabric unaided to complete the embroidered design.

If your Fab Lab doesn't have a sewing machine of any kind, ask the manager or technical guru if basic craft materials are available. You can still do a lot with a needle, conductive thread, LED lights, and an idea.

CUT FROM THE SAME CLOTH

At the textile workstation, you may find other machines and equipment. Some of the common tools used in project construction are scissors, seam rippers, a mannequin for draping and fitting, or a pincushion filled with pins and needles. You may also notice tools specifically for the digital sewing machine, such as embroidery hoops and stabilizers. Embroidery hoops or frames keep the fabric stretched tight while the machine embroiders. Stabilizers are used to support the fabric under the embroidery work. After the design is finished, the stabilizers are torn away or rinsed off with water.

Other textile machines found in a Fab Lab are sergers and knitting machines. A serger can cut a seam and lay an overstitch on the raw edge all in one move, producing a finished edge. The machine simultaneously uses four spools of thread to create an overlock stitch. A CNC knitting machine weaves horizontally and knits textiles with interconnecting loops of yarn. It can produce projects with complex 3D shapes and geometric knits. A less common machine found in the lab is a 3D sewing machine. Working just like a 3D printer, the sewing machine uses yarn instead of plastic and prints on soft surfaces such as felt fabric.

If your local Fab Lab is interested in expanding their textile workstation, check out the digital knitting machine OpenKnit.

(continued on the next page)

(continued from the previous page)

It's an open-source, low cost digital fabrication tool. Using a 3D printer, hardware, and paper clips, the OpenKnit machine can be built inside a Fab Lab! The machine can knit beanies, sweaters, and scarves. Find complete instructions on the Instructables website.

Not Your Grandma's Embroidery

With all the cool textile machines in Fab Labs, the project possibilities are numerous and diverse. Although a mechanical sewing machine can't produce fancy stitches or embroidery, it can assist in making just about any project. Open-source patterns are available for beginner projects that will take only a few hours. Find a project, print and cut pattern pieces to create a bag for books, a cell phone pouch, or a hot beverage sleeve. Spruce up the project with conductive thread and LED lights.

An electronic sewing machine provides decorative stitching options and advanced settings for better stitching control. Projects that require a bit more stitching precision are easier and more manageable. Create a skateboard sling or a bike caddy with pockets for everything. Does Buddy the dog need a new collar? Fashion a new adjustable collar to go with his next Halloween costume. Add glow-in-the-dark thread and you will be able to spot him during nighttime walks.

When thinking of embroidery projects, do you picture grandma's pillows? They might be beautiful but not really your style. Pillows are nice, but it is time to update the idea of

Embellish a personalized embroidered design with sewable electronic pieces, such as LilyPad Arduino. Using conductive thread and LED lights, you can program the design to light up and blink.

embroidery. With a digital sewing machine, you can use designs as a way to personalize anything. Bring in a t-shirt from your closet and embroider a favorite quote. Pick out a tiny embroidered design and mount it onto a necklace pendant. Or turn an intricate embroidered lace pattern into a masquerade mask. For any sewing project chosen, whether it is a simply sewn bookmark or complicated embroidered t-shirt, the fabricator can add spice with a conductive thread and LED lights.

Wearing More Than One Hat

Sitting at the textile workstation, you are holding conductive thread in one hand and scissors in the other. Now what? You're stoked to get creating but totally stumped on where to begin or what to make. Inspiration can be found in many ways. A great place to start is in the Fab Lab. Spend time in the lab, observing and talking to other users. Ask what they are making and why. Fab Labs are public invention workshops. Project ideas can come from many places—curiosity, an itch to solve a problem, or a desire to explore creativity. Walk around the lab and investigate

Be inspired by the many colorful reels of embroidery thread and the range of vibrant designs that can be created.

different workstations. Figure out which technologies you'd like to use and start from there.

Other brainstorming activities include creating an inspiration board or collage. Flip through magazines, newspapers, and books for ideas. See something cool, such as a design or color? Clip it out and stick it on a collage or board. Also research online and collect interesting and inspiring projects. Some great websites to bookmark are Pinterest, Instructables, or the Adafruit wearables page. You can also browse past Fab Lab textile projects on Fabshare and the eTextile Lounge.

Look inside your own closet for ideas. Do you have a favorite sweatshirt that could use some sprucing up with a design and lights? Or perhaps there is a t-shirt you don't wear anymore because it's too small but you still love the t-shirt's design. How can you salvage the old and create something new? If you can't find anything in your closet, head to a local thrift store for ideas and textiles.

Still stumped? Step outside and take a look around. Observing nature and the environment is an excellent way to find inspiration. In fact, the US Navy took a cue from a bottlenose dolphin's triangular wings when designing a more efficient wing for passenger jets and fighter planes. Burdock burrs inspired a Swiss engineer to develop the handy invention of Velcro. Finding design solutions inspired by nature is called biomimicry. Fab Labs are full of problem solvers, inventors, and designers. The key to finding innovation is to think outside the box.

Chapter
THREE

EDUCATION AND SKILLS

fter spending time in the Fab Lab chatting with others and researching, you finally decide to engineer a wickedly cool Halloween costume. Thrilled with the possibilities, you can already envision the enormous bag of candy you will score for inventiveness and creativity. You have the idea, what is the next step? Time to get your hands dirty and start fabricating.

Roll Up Your Sleeves

Every great invention begins with an idea. After brainstorming, it's time to put the concept on paper. Sketch out a design and prototype for the project. A prototype is an original or first model of a project that is revised and further developed. Begin by writing down the project components, criteria, and constraints. Make a list of needed materials and which machines will be used. In a Fab Lab, users are not limited to one machine. Nor are they

Put your ideas on paper. Using markers and colored pencils, draft a prototype of your project. Sketch out details and different possibilities.

limited to building a project one certain way. List steps from starting point to completion and any obstacles that may arise during production. If you are unsure where to start, find similar projects and take note of each step. Or talk to your Fab Lab community and ask for advice or suggestions.

After creating a work plan for the project, follow the plan and build it. If you have decided to create a personal embroidered design, you will need to draft the image on paper first and then move it into a digital format. Most Fab Labs will have 2D vector design programs available. Inkscape is free open-source vector graphics software and is great for creating illustrations and logos. Tutorials are available if needed. Other vector design programs you may see in the lab are Adobe Illustrator or SketchUp.

Most digital sewing machines can read a CSD or PES file. But vector design programs, like Inkscape and Illustrator, cannot save the file as a PES. Not to worry though, digitizer programs will convert the file so the embroidery design can speak the language of the digital sewing machine. Open-source digitizer software is available, such as Thredworks or SophieSew. The software converts the vector image into an editable stitching format that includes embroidering-specific information such as thread color and stitching lines. If your Fab Lab doesn't have converter software, talk with the technical guru or lab manager about downloading an open-source program. Another option is using an all-in-one software program such as Stitch Era Universal. It is free embroidery software that enables the user to design a vector drawing right in the program, convert the file, and send it to the digital sewing machine. Digital sewing machines also come with preloaded designs that are adjustable. The embroidery selection is wide and varied and includes different fonts and frame pattern combinations.

Using a digitizer software program, convert a vector image into a sewable embroidered design. The translated file will guide the digital sewing machine to produce an original embroidered work.

The project is constructed, but you decide that it needs just a bit more. You want it to shine, literally. At the electronic and hardware workstation, you will find tools used to insert LEDs and batteries into the fabric. Common electronic kits found in Fab Labs are KiCAD, Arduino, and Eagle. Arduino is most commonly used with e-textiles and is relatively easy to learn. It is an open-source prototyping platform based on user-friendly hardware and software. Arduino kits include sensors, switches, LED lights, and microcontrollers or programmable circuit boards. The microcontroller works as the brains of a project, telling the circuit board to follow a set of instructions, such as turning on an LED light or activating a sensor. Depending on the project, microcontroller boards can be programmed to do whatever you desire. The Arduino programming language and software are based on easy to learn programs aimed at users without previous electronics or programming experience. The Arduino website also offers tutorials, troubleshooting tips, and reference guides about getting started with their hardware and software. Source code is available to insert into several projects. Or if you're interested in learning code or programming, these platforms provide an accessible opportunity.

After inserting a microcontroller programmed to set your LEDs to blink, you step back and admire your first prototype. Congratulations! Celebrate the success of bringing an idea through to fruition. The next step is refining the prototype. After evaluating the project, maybe the design is a bit wonky or perhaps the LEDs do not flash as intended. Can you make it better or use a more appropriate material? Or can the design improve to ensure durability or adjustability? Tinker with the construction. Try different materials. Ask questions of the concept and find new solutions.

"Celebrate the successful creation of your project with others. Fab Labs are all about sharing experiences, collaborating on ideas, and learning from the global network of users.

Once you've crafted the best version of your project, share it with others. Offer tips about what worked and didn't work. Note the challenges, and highlight areas where other users can insert their own style and preference. Sharing projects is a defining unique quality of Fab Labs. It's about celebrating and learning from each other in a collaborative and supportive workspace.

Under Your Belt

One of the great aspects about Fab Labs is the ability to walk in without previous engineering, design, or sewing experience and be able to make (almost) anything. But if showing up in the lab without any previous knowledge makes you a little nervous, there are many resources available to give you a head start.

Does your school offer textile classes? Research if there is an after-school club or organization that you could join. Investigate community education, too. Sewing classes are often available for a low cost. Or if you have a sewing machine at home, educational opportunities are available online, such as Craftsy's free basic sewing classes. With free beginner tutorials, you can learn sewing construction fundamentals. Also check out basic sewing books from the library.

Perhaps the "e-" part of e-textiles kind of freaks you out. Not to worry. Adafruit replaces the fear with fun. Their website offers almost two hundred different e-textile tutorials, all using Arduino toolkits that can be found in Fab Labs. Learn about the anatomy of LEDs and how to control their brightness with voltage or resistors. Or master how to chose the right battery to power your project.

Do the other machines in the lab intimidate you? Fab Connect, Fab Academy, and the Fab Foundation all provide basic introductions to the different machines and software found

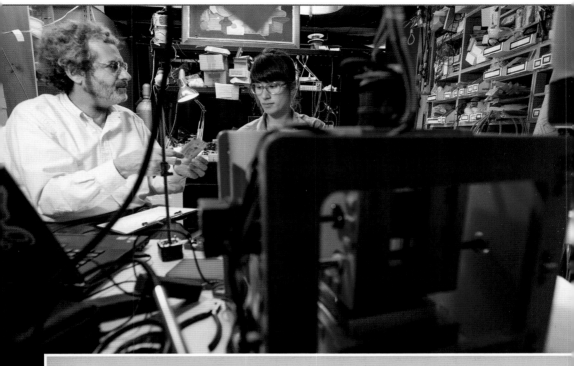

At the Massachusetts Institute of Technology's Center for Bits and Atoms, Neil Gershenfeld researches how to turn data into things and supports the global network of Fab Labs.

in Fab Labs across the world. Written and video tutorials are available. Also, remember that you can hang out in a Fab Lab before jumping into a project. Talk with other users and ask how the machines work. Fab Labs are educational shared work spaces, and most users are eager to share their knowledge.

On the Same Wavelength

If you're ready to take your Fab Lab experience to the next level, explore the different festivals, conferences, and community events held around the world. It's a great avenue for meeting other users and discovering new projects.

SUMMER CAMPS

Have too many activities during the school year to commit to invention? Fab Lab summer camps are available. Located on the University of Illinois campus, the Champaign-Urbana Community Fab Lab offers several summer workshops and camps. Camp Fab Lab is a weeklong adventure through all the different workstations, including an introduction to e-textiles and digital embroidery. Camp Fab Lab II is a weeklong design workshop for the more experienced user. Campers fabricate in teams to design a prototype that meets a challenge or solves a problem. The teams present their projects in the final-day showcase. Another summer camp located in Sarasota, Florida, the Suncoast Science Faulhaber Fab Lab hosts a girls-only class called Design Squad. Participants learn to create laser-cut fashion accessories and LED necklaces. The lab also offers an Awesome Arduino class for users new to electronics. Participants build interactive lights that respond to touch.

If there aren't any summer camps offered in your area, look into virtual Maker Camps. Maker Camp is a free online community for creators interested in learning, tinkering, and connecting with others. Campers can make projects, take virtual field trips to camps across the world, and interact with other campers and counselors. To see if there is a Maker Camp in your neighborhood, check out their website.

Each year the international Fab Lab community meets somewhere different. The Fab 2014 International Conference and festival was held in Barcelona, Spain. The event offered a workshop for teaching kids how to make an interactive shirt using conductive paint. In 2015, the cities of Boston, Cambridge, and Somerville hosted the International Fab Lab Conference and Symposium. The event included talks, educational seminars, workshops, and interactive activities. During the Fab Festival, a public event held the same weekend, a Fab Fashion Show exhibited the latest in wearable technologies, such as interactive clothing for musicians and dancers.

The United States Fab Lab Network holds its own event, an annual symposium. It is a packed three-day event full of workshops, exhibits, and presentations on education and building a Fab Lab in your community. Ticket price is in the hundreds but includes a membership to the network, and academic rates are available. If you're looking to rub elbows with the top names and industry experts in smart textiles and wearable technology, check out the WEAR Conference. Past attendees include Google, Apple, Adidas, Nike, Patagonia, and Intel. The event features presentations, keynote speakers, tours, and workshops.

Check with your local college or university for other events. If the institution has a design or fashion program, investigate if they are experimenting with wearable technology. Students will often organize a public event to showcase their projects. Kent State University's Fashion School hosts an annual Fashion/ Tech Hackathon weekend, at which students from all majors collaborate to create a project. The event is free and high school students can participate. A Fab Lab experience is all about connecting and learning from others, and these events are great ways to do that.

Chapter
FOUR

PROJECTS

So far you've learned the history of Fab Labs, discovered the functions of a digital sewing machine, and how to create a work plan for a project. Now it's time to poke your needle into fabricating. In this section, you will find a description, materials list, and tips for beginner, immediate, and advanced projects. Variations on the projects are available on several open-source platforms.

Bookmark Light

Reading in the dark has never been so much fun as with a bookmark light. This beginner project is a great introduction to using electronics and textiles. The bookmark can be constructed without a sewing machine by using just a needle and thread. Decorate the bookmark with markers or cut out pieces of felt. The time needed for the project is two to four hours. Programming is not required. For step-by-step instructions, check out the book *Sew Electric* from your local library.

Several project resources can be found at your local library. Search the shelves for books on sewing, design, and e-textiles.

Materials and tools:
- Paper to make your bookmark pattern
- Scissors
- Glue
- Colored pencils or markers
- Chalk for marking fabric
- One or two felt pieces or any stiff fabric like denim
- Sewing needle
- Coin cell battery
- Coin cell battery holder
- LED light

● Conductive thread

Project tips: While designing your bookmark, be mindful of your circuit design. Make sure to use a parallel connection. Connect the correct ends together, positive (+) with the positive (+), and the negative (-) with the negative (-). Also remember to keep the positive (+) and negative (-) circuit thread lines away from each other, and make sure that they do not touch. If they do connect, even in the slightest, it will cause a short circuit and damage the battery.

LED Wristband

With LED lights, your personalized wristband will shine with style. This beginner project can be assembled with a needle and thread. But if you'd like to embellish your wristband with a pre-loaded embroidered design, the digital sewing machine can also be used for this project. Or you can keep it simple and decorate the wristband with felt pieces, buttons, markers, or anything that represents your style. The project requires three to four hours of time, depending on your wristband design. Programming is not needed. There are several variations of this project available on the Instructables website.

Materials and tools:
● Paper to make your wristband pattern
● Scissors
● Glue
● Colored markers
● Buttons or other embellishments
● Chalk for marking fabric

The LED wristband can be made with a variety of firm but flexible materials such as felt, soft leather, or brocade fabric.

- Ruler tape
- One or two felt pieces
- Sewing needle
- Coin cell battery
- Coin cell battery holder
- LED light
- Conductive thread
- Hole snap
- Prong snap

Project tips: The snap works as the on/off switch. Make sure to sew the hole snap on the back of the wristband, hole facing out. Measure your wrist with the ruler tape to ensure a great fit. If you decide to embroider a design, attach a stabilizer to the back of the felt for support. After it is embroidered, peel off the stabilizer. Love your design? Make more! Wristbands are a great way to show support for different causes.

Blinking Backpack Patch

Light up your path and travel safely at night with a blinking backpack patch. This intermediate project uses a digital sewing machine to make the patch. Choose from a preloaded design or create your own. This project requires you to use code to program the LED blinking lights, but the source code is available for download. You can fabricate this project in three to five hours. For step-by-step written and video instructions, check out the Maker Media website.

Materials and tools:
- Fabric to embroider
- Extra fabric for the backing and patch border
- Patch design
- Embroidery stabilizer
- Embroidery floss
- Embroidery hoop
- A backpack or bag
- Scissors
- Needle-nose pliers
- Sewing needle
- Conductive thread

- Conductive Velcro
- Regular Velcro
- Twelve LED lights in your choice of color
- LiPower board
- LilyPad AA battery holder
- LilyPad Arduino with programmer and USB cable
- Source code and schematic

Project tips: Attach the patch to your backpack using regular Velcro for easy removal at the airport or on a rainy day. Create a backing and border around your patch to give it a nice finished look. Check your power supply before finalizing the project so you can adjust and fix any problems. You can also substitute the LilyPad AAA battery holder with a lithium-polymer battery and charger.

Chessboard and 3D Pieces

If you're a chess nut, you are going to love this portable, personalized chessboard set. Using the sewing machine and

Built from the ground up, 3D-printed chess pieces are durable and will outlast even the toughest competitor. Choose from a wide selection of designs at Thingiverse.

3D printer, you can create a custom game board and pieces. A chessboard is a simple design—sixty-four squares in eight rows and eight columns. Budget at least a week or two to construct this intermediate project, with the sixteen chess pieces taking the longest to build. Each chess piece could take up to two hours to 3D-print. Several open-source 3D chess piece designs are available, ranging from very simple to very complex. There is even a set modeled after Minecraft characters that was designed by a class! For chess piece ideas and digital files, check out the Thingiverse website.

Materials and tools:
- Paper to make pattern for chessboard
- Ruler
- Two yards of cotton fabric in two different colors or patterns for the sixty-four squares
- Two different colors of ABS or PLA plastic. Amount will vary depending on the scale size of chess pieces and design.
- Sewing machine
- Sewing pins
- Scissors
- Needle and thread
- Chess piece design digital file

Project tips: While hanging out at the textile station, search for scrap fabric and create a simple travel bag for your game. Or reuse scrap materials for the squares of your chessboard. For the chess pieces, make sure to scale to size depending on the size of the chessboard. Don't want to wait for 3D printed chess pieces? Create 2D fabric pieces with embroidered chess designs.

MAKE YOURSELF AT HOME

If you don't have access to a Fab Lab or if your lab doesn't have a textile workstation, simple e-textile projects are available to make at home. Glow-in-the-dark thread can liven up any t-shirt, backpack, or blanket. The thread glows without an electrical source. Simply hold the thread up to any light for thirty seconds and it will illuminate for hours. But keep it out of the dryer and away from irons. Glow thread is relatively inexpensive and can be found in most fabric stores.

Electroluminescent wire, or EL wire, is a bendable wire coated with phosphor and covered with PVC. It lights up like neon and is easy to use with many different projects. It's a cold wire, which means it does not generate heat, and is safe to wear. But the wire does require a power source through an inverter and batteries. Insert EL wire into a hat or computer bag. Adafruit's website offers an open-source glowing EL wire beanbag project, good for nighttime yard games. You can also purchase the wire from their website.

E-textile toolkits are available for purchase and home delivery, or you can build your own kit. Your toolkit should include conductive thread, sewable battery holders, LED lights, coin cell batteries, and a needle to get the work done. The project possibilities are infinite. Dig through last season's winter gear and get to work on updating your style with a little glimmer and glam.

Illuminated Constellation Embroidery

Learn astronomy while embroidering your favorite night sky constellation! Pick a canvas to embellish and a constellation, and never miss a light show again. This interactive advanced project sparkles and flashes when you move. Use the constellation as the main design on a t-shirt, skirt, or bag. Does your birthday fall between July 22 and August 22? Make a Leo the Lion constellation. Or pair up the Big and Little Dipper for a more complex design. Draft the pattern in Inkscape or find an open-source constellation image and convert the file. This advanced project will take five to six hours for construction. For a project tutorial, electrical guides, and programming source code, go to Adafruit's wearables webpage.

Materials and tools:
- Pattern for chosen constellation and night sky
- FLORA main board
- FLORA accelerometer and compass module
- 12 FLORA RGB NeoPixels
- 150mAh LiPo battery or 3xAAA battery pack
- Basic multimeter
- Conductive thread
- Standard thread
- T-shirt, skirt, or bag to embroider
- Clear nail polish to seal knots
- Embroidery marker or tailor's chalk
- Scissors
- Sewing needle
- Source code and schematic

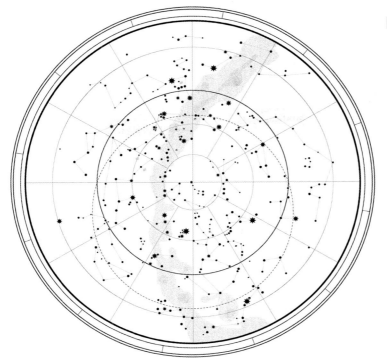

Open-source vector images of the night sky are available, such as this astronomical celestial map of the Northern Hemisphere. Or select a favorite constellation to embroider.

Project tips: Use an embroidery hoop to stabilize the circuit and support the fabric while you sew. It will make the task a lot easier and produce a more finished look. On a budget but still want your stars to shine? Buy a battery-powered LED string of lights. Insert the lights into your constellation project.

Mystical LED Halloween Hood

Fabricate a wickedly spooky Halloween costume using a sewing machine, 3D printer, and LEDs. The mystical LED Halloween hood has glowing red eyes. The glowing LEDs are sewn into a translucent black fabric face panel to give it an extra creepy appearance. The costume is perfect for dressing as a Jawa from

Star Wars or Dementor from *Harry Potter*. Or revamp a Little Red Riding Hood costume into Little Red Terror. The time required for this advanced project is around five to six hours. For step by step instructions, programming source code, and the hood pattern, go to Adafruit's wearables webpage.

Materials and tools:
- Two NeoPixel Jewels
- Arduino GEMMA microcontroller
- Silicone-coated stranded wire (30awg recommended)
- Soldering tools and supplies
- Sewing pins
- Tailor's chalk
- 19awg galvanized steel wire
- Two yards of heavy fabric for hood/cape
- One yard of translucent fabric for face panel
- Sewing machine
- Scissors
- Needle and thread
- Flexible 3D-printing filament
- Source code and schematic

Project tips: Decorate the hood with your own embellishments; attach embroidered lace or use scrap fabric found at the textile station. Fasten 3D-printed horns for extra eeriness. The 3D-printed battery holder is great for other wearable projects. Be forewarned, you will be the envy of all your friends. You may bring home more Halloween candy than expected, which could result in mandatory sharing with parents or siblings.

Chapter FIVE

BIG PICTURE

No longer science fiction fantasy, high-tech textiles are illuminating fashion runways and accessorizing our arms, ears, and more. Wearable technology takes the function of fashion to the extremes. From smart headbands that analyze sweat to earbuds that hush the sound of a screaming toddler, wearable tech is exploring the possibilities and then reaching beyond. Inside Fab Labs, users are learning the skills to imagine the future of high-tech fashion.

Melon is a smart headband that reads and tracks a user's brainwaves during different activities, such as studying or playing sports.

Having an Ace Up Your Sleeve

Little did you know, after spending hours, days, and weeks in the Fab Lab, you were mastering valuable skills that can be added to your toolbox of knowledge. Inside each produced project is a multitude of lessons learned that could benefit you in the future.

Brainstorming encourages creative problem solving and thinking outside the box. Fab Labs are renowned for cracking common or unusual problems. Need a 3D printer for the new lab, but don't have the cash? A project called EWaste 60$ 3D printer was a finalist for the 2015 Global Creative Awards during the International Fab Lab Conference. The project built a low-budget 3D printer out of recycled electronic components. The skills learned while inventing a solution to a problem can help you tackle any future challenge.

Once an idea is planted, it needs instructions on how to grow and bring it to fruition. The invaluable skill of translating a concept and communicating it to others is needed across a variety of fields, such as health care, climate science, and engineering. Fab Labs give users the opportunity to hone their communication skills by fabricating from scratch and sharing the projects with others. Deconstructing a concept is also part of the project process in a Fab Lab, and an opportunity to build a skill. Each step taken in a project is a possibility for reinvention and improvement. Understanding how a product is made shines light on its life cycle. This knowledge can quickly morph into curiosity and the next thing you know, you will be taking things apart just to see how they're put together.

It takes curiosity to step inside a room full of industrial-grade machines and use computer programs to tinker and bring your idea to life. But it takes perseverance to keeping working and perfect a project prototype. A skill not easily learned, determination is the result of focus, motivation, and good old-fashioned stick-to-it-ness. Working on projects inside the Fab Lab can teach you a lot about perseverance. But remember: the sum of the whole is greater than the parts. You are not alone in a Fab Lab. Your Fab Lab community is there to support and conspire with you. Collaboration is key to unlocking the ability to play many different roles and connect with many different people. Communication, collaboration, perseverance, and many more skills can be used in life, whether you might be designing the latest wearable for Google or guiding the next generation of Fab Lab users.

Wearing Your Heartbeat on Your Sleeve

The wearable revolution is making daily life a little easier and workplaces a lot safer. According to the US Department of Labor, more than four thousand construction workers were killed on the job in 2014. The most common causes of injury or death are falls, electrocutions, being struck by an object or being caught in between machinery. The men and women who help build our cities and homes need protection.

Revamping the already mandatory uniform of a hardhat and vest, two kinds of wearables are being tested on job sites—the smart safety vest and the smart hardhat. Both items provide valuable information and help prevent injury. The smart hardhat can detect if the wearer falls or is struck by an object. It will notify and report the injury. The smart safety vest can connect to a mobile interface that shows the wearer's location, vitals, body temperature, and any repetitive motion, which can reveal injuries. This is just the beginning of increased safety in the workplace.

MADE TO MEASURE

Wearable technology makes our clothes earn their keep. High-tech fashion is not only creative, but also functional. The massive tech company Google is collaborating with the iconic denim company Levi Strauss & Co to bring an updated version of a classic. Project Jacquard is experimenting with creating mass-market interactive e-textile products that are constructed with conductive yarns and embedded with electronics no bigger than a button. The next pair of Levi jeans you buy may have the capacity to silence your phone with a simple swipe of a pocket.

Moving from jean pockets to earbuds, another tech company is seeking to augment the soundscape with a new

The Swedish company Earin has created wireless earbuds that synch with a smartphone and provide hours of high-precision sound. Small and light, the earbuds weigh less than a nickel.

wearable device. Here Active Listening transforms the audio world with two wireless earbuds and a smartphone app. The rechargeable earbuds can alter the acoustics in a room with poor quality sound or turn down the volume of a screaming baby. They use Bluetooth technology to connect wirelessly to a smartphone, where the user can adjust the settings through an app. Like a stereographic equalizer used to edit music, the app can adjust the volume, bass, or treble. In the near future, Here Active Listening might even enable translation of live speech.

Wearable technology is a rapidly growing and innovative field, especially with the Internet of Things revolution. The Internet of Things is a connected network of objects, such as wearables, that can communicate to each other. Using the internet to send and receive data, a sensor in your smart sweater notes that your body temperature is lower than normal, and sends a notice to the smart thermostat to kick on the heat. Or your fitness tracker reads your biometrics and senses a nasty cold coming on. It then sends a note to your doctor and adds oranges to the grocery list. Synching wearables to the Internet of Things ecosystem is already happening in the high-tech fashion industry.

Another wearable that is working to save lives, money, and time is the Vital Connect's HealthPatch MD. This biosensor patch can be used for outpatient care in the comfort of a patient's home. The patch monitors heart rate, respiratory rate, body temperature, and detects if the wearer has fallen down. HealthPatch MD has Bluetooth capabilities and can connect to a mobile device to retrieve real-time data. The doctor can monitor and guide a patient's treatment.

Functional and stylish, the Apple Watch notifies a user of incoming texts, emails, and calendar events. The smartwatch also tracks daily activity and fitness goals.

Wearables not only monitor sickness and injury, but they can also track fitness and health. FitBit, Jawbone, and Apple Watch are just a few of the popular fitness trackers that are counting users' steps and sleep patterns. But scientists are investigating a smart wristband or headband that reads sweat. Sweat is loaded with chemical data. A doctor can use sweat to diagnose some diseases, track levels of glucose, and even detect high levels of lead. Sweat sensor smart wristbands could help athletes optimize their performance or help a doctor diagnose a disease or ailment without invasively poking and prodding the body. Emerging wearable technology in health care is a growing and profitable market.

IF THE SHOE FITS, WEAR IT

Wearable technology is moving beyond trend and will be an essential part of our everyday lives in the near future. There will be a call for engineers, designers, and programmers to help develop the next generation of new wearables.

From textile designers to software developers, the opportunities in wearable technology are varied. The industry is at the intersection of fashion, function, and technology. Electrical and computer engineers are needed to building the platforms that will communicate with clothes. Textile designers will understand how the computer components can be integrated into current textiles construction. Material scientists study the durability and safety of e-materials and help engineers select the best for new applications. Smart fabrics are not just for wearables. Interior designers are using e-textiles to channel light or heat to specific parts of a room.

Universities offer degrees in textile design, electrical engineering, computer science, and apparel studies—all of which can prepare you for a career in wearable technology. Big-name companies such as Google, Nike, and Intel are all experimenting with the possibilities of e-textiles. Depending on where your interests lie, a degree will help you score a job in this innovative and emergent field. But why wait until college to prep? Start now with the tools, software, and ideas inside a Fab Lab. The experience and skills developed while tinkering with e-textiles in the lab will give you a leg up over the rest.

Pushing the Envelope

High-tech product prototyping doesn't happen only inside corporate boardrooms and industrial factories. Whether your dream is to engineer a space suit for NASA or design a smart shirt for Olympic athletes, Fabrication Laboratories are a great place to begin experimenting with wearable technology. Fab Labs provide opportunities to test theories, explore ideas, and build a concept up from scratch. Inside the lab, you become a fashion

During a preseason friendly soccer match between Oxford United and West Ham United, a player wears a Catapult vest. The smart wearable vest monitors the athlete's exertion and fitness.

designer, engineer, and inventor all in one. It is a place where you can sit at a table with friends (or strangers) and troubleshoot a design problem or applaud a recent success. Fab Labs are all of this and more.

Looking into the future, two things are clear—humans (and some domestic pets) will continue to wear clothes and accessories every day. And second, technology will continue to connect us in many ways. Wearable technology could become the next greatest thing since smartphones or sewing machines. Imagine coming home from school and your smartwatch signals the door's smartlock to unlock as you arrive. Inside, you set down your sensor-embedded backpack that alerts the kitchen that you are home and ready for a snack; the toaster oven begins to crisp up a slice of cinnamon toast. Your fitness tracker detects that you're a little dehydrated and messages the fridge to pour you a cold glass of water. As you sit down to relax and enjoy your grub, you swipe your jean pocket to activate the playlist on your phone. The music begins to beat from the speakers inside your sweatshirt's hood. Envision the possibilities with the future of wearable technology. And then head to the Fab Lab and start fabricating.

Glossary

biomimicry Using design solutions and processes inspired by nature.

bobbin A spool wound with thread used in sewing machines.

conductive textiles Fabric made with metal threads, such as copper, silver, or aluminum, that can conduct electricity.

digital fabrication Building a product using a variety of materials and computer-controlled machines.

digital sewing machine Also called a computerized sewing machine, a machine that sews a variety of utility and decorative stitches, including embroidery. It can connect to a computer.

digitizer software A software program that converts a vector file into a digital embroidery file suitable for a digital sewing machine.

electric circuit A closed path in which an electrical current flows.

EL wire Short for "electroluminescent wire," a flexible wire coated with phosphor that glows with electric current.

embroidery A decorative and detailed design sewn into fabric either by hand or with a digital sewing machine.

embroidery hoop A frame used to keep fabric stretched and taut while embroidering.

Internet of Things A connected network of physical objects that sends and receives data through sensors and the internet.

LED Short for "light-emitting diode," a bulb containing electroluminescent material that lights up with an electrical current.

open-source software Computer software or source code that can be used, altered, and distributed to the public.

pattern A template of the different pieces used to construct a fabric project. The pattern pieces are pinned to fabric, cut out, and then sewn together.

PES file A file that contains the embroidery pattern layout and color design instructions for a digital sewing machine.

prototype An original or first model of a project that is revised and further developed.

soldering A metal that melts with low heat. It's used for connecting electronic wires.

soldering iron A tool to melt solder and connect electronics.

stabilizer A support used to secure fabric while embroidering that is removed after the stitching is complete.

wearable technology Electronic devices that can be worn on the body, either as clothing made with conductive textiles or as accessories.

Association of Sewing and Design Professionals, Inc.
2885 Sanford Ave SW #19588
Grandville, MI 49418
(877) 755-0303
Website: http://www.sewingprofessionals.org/
The Association of Sewing and Design Professionals is a network of dressmakers, seamstresses, and garment designers in the United States and Canada. The network encourages and supports students in fashion design.

Canada Science and Technology Museums Corporation
PO Box 9724, Station T
Ottawa, Ontario K1G 5A3
(866) 442-4416
Website: http://techno-science.ca
The Canada Science and Technology Museums Corporation is a comprehensive science and technology institution that promotes and celebrates Canada's scientific and technological heritage.

Center for Bits and Atoms
Massachusetts Institute of Technology
IT Room E15-401
20 Ames Street
Cambridge, MA 02139
(617) 253-0392
Website: http://cba.mit.edu
The Center for Bits and Atoms at MIT is an interdisciplinary enterprise exploring the relationship between computer science bits and physical science atoms.

Fab Foundation
50 Milk Street, 16th Floor
Boston, MA 02109
(857) 333-7777
Website: www.fabfoundation.org
The Fab Foundation provides support to the growing
    international Fab Lab network through education and
    development resources.

Million Women Mentors (MWM)
1200 New Hampshire Avenue NW, Suite 820
Washington, DC 20036
(202) 296-9222
Website: http://www.millionwomenmentors.org
Million Women Mentors is a network of one million mentors
    that encourage girls and women to pursue STEM programs
    and careers.

TAF Academy
26720 40th Avenue S
Kent, WA 98032
(253) 945-5187
Website: http://techaccess.org/academy
TAF Academy is a sixth to twelfth grade STEM public school
    that prepares students for careers in science, technology,
    engineering, and math. The school has a project-based
    curriculum.

Toronto Fashion Incubator
285 Manitoba Drive
Exhibition Place

Toronto, ON, Canada, M6K 3C3

(416) 971-7117

Website: http://www.fashionincubator.com

The Toronto Fashion Incubator is an award-winning nonprofit organization that supports and mentors Canadian fashion designers and entrepreneurs.

Websites

Because of the changing nature of internet links, Rosen Publishing has developed an online list of websites related to the subject of this book. This site is updated regularly. Please use this link to access this list:

http://www.rosenlinks.com/GCFL/sew

Buechley, Leah. *Textile Messages: Dispatches from the World of E-Textiles and Education.* New York, NY: Peter Lang Pub Incorporated, 2013.

Buechley, Leah, and Kanjun Qiu. *Sew Electric: A Collection of DIY Projects that Combine Fabric, Electronics, and Programming.* Cambridge, MA: HLT Press, 2013.

Führer, Mia. *Upcycle Your Wardrobe: 21 Sewing Projects for Unique, New Fashions.* Atglen, PA: Schiffer Publishing, 2015.

Hartman, Kate. *Make: Wearable Electronics: Design, Prototype, and Wear Your Own Interactive Garments.* San Francisco, CA: Maker Media, Incorporated, 2014.

Haynes, Christine. *The Complete Photo Guide to Clothing Construction.* Minneapolis, MN: Creative Publishing International, 2014.

Lang, David. *Zero to Maker: Learn (Just Enough) to Make (Just About) Anything.* San Francisco, CA: Maker Media, Inc., 2013.

McEwen, Adrian. *Designing the Internet of Things.* Hoboken, NJ: John Wiley & Sons, 2013.

Mortenson, Melissa. *Project Teen: Handmade Gifts Your Teen Will Love.* Concord, CA: C&T Publishing Inc, 2014.

Stewart, Becky. *Adventures in Arduino.* Hoboken, NJ: John Wiley & Sons, 2015.

Swanson, Jennifer A. *The Wonderful World of Wearable Devices.* New York, NY: Rosen Publishing Group, 2015.

Toth-Chernin, Jan. *E-Textiles.* North Mankato MN: Cherry Lake Publishing, 2013.

For Further Reading

Bibliography

Adafruit Industries. "Learn Wearables." Retrieved February 22, 2016 https://learn.adafruit.com/category/wearables.

Barrett, John. "The Internet of Things: Where the Web and the physical world will meet." TEDx Talks CIT, October 5, 2012. https://www.youtube.com/watch?v=QaTIt1C5R-M.

Buechley, Leah, and Kanjun Qiu. *E-Textiles-in-a-Box tutorial.* National Center for Women and Information Technology, May 5, 2014. http://www.ncwit.org/etextiles.

Cavalcanti, Gui. "Is it a Hackerspace, Makerspace, TechShop or FabLab?" Makezine, May 22, 2013. http://makezine.com/2013/05/22/the-difference-between-hackerspaces-makerspaces-techshops-and-fablabs/.

Choi, Charles Q. "Fine-Tune the World with 'Augmented Reality' Earbuds." Live Science, February 4, 2016. http://www.livescience.com/53599-augmented-reality-here-earbuds.html.

Choi, Charles Q. "Wearable Sweat Sensors Could Track Your Health." Live Science, January 27, 2016. http://www.livescience.com/53499-wearable-sweat-sensors-track-health.html.

Eng, Diana. *Fashion Geek: Clothes Accessories Tech.* New York, NY: North Light Books, 2009.

Fab Foundation. "The Fab Charter." Retrieved February 24, 2016. http://www.fabfoundation.org/about-us.

Fab Foundation. "Setting up a Fab Lab." Retrieved February 24, 2016. http://www.fabfoundation.org/fab-labs/setting-up-a-fab-lab.

Gershenfeld, Neil. "Unleash your creativity in a Fab Lab." TED Talk Conference, February 2006. https://www.ted.com/talks/neil_gershenfeld_on_fab_labs?language=en.

Hastings, Pamela J. *Creative Sewing Projects withComputerized Machines.* New York, NY: Sterling Pub Co Inc, 1997.

Hwang, Victor W. "How Does Silicon Valley Teach Its Children with a Fab Lab!" Forbes, August 7, 2013. http://www.forbes.com.

Midwest Digital Fabrication Partnership. "Fab Lab Introduction Guide." Edition 3, Revision 2, 2011. http://dflcusa.org/downloads/introduction.pdf.

Olsson, Tony. "Open Softwear: Fashionable prototyping and wearable computing using the Arduino." Creative Commons, 2008. http://softwear.cc/book/files/Open_Softwear-beta090712.pdf.

Pakhchyan, Syuzi. *Fashioning Technology: A DIY Intro to Smart Crafting.* Newton, MA: O'Reilly Media, Inc., 2008.

Pierce, David. "Google is Hacking our Clothes to Work Like Touchscreens." Wired, May 29, 2015. http://www.wired.com/2015/05/google-wants-turn-everything-wearable.

Salomone, Andrew. "Conductive Fabric for Soft Circuits." Makezine. January 16, 2013. http://makezine.com/2013/01/16/conductive-fabric-for-soft-circuits.

SparkFun Electronics. "Sewing with Conductive Thread." Retrieved February 22, 2016. https://learn.sparkfun.com/tutorials/sewing-with-conductive-thread.

Index

About the Author

Kristina Lyn Heitkamp is a Montana-based writer, researcher, and science journalist. She has been fabricating with a mechanical sewing machine since she was 12 years old, when she made her first Halloween costume, a red-fringed 1920's flapper dress. She is a freelance researcher for National Geographic Books and a contributor to the children's magazines *Odyssey*, *Muse*, and *Faces*.

Photo Credits

Cover Moreno Soppelsa/Shutterstock.com; pp. 4–5 Champaign Urbana Community Fab Lab; p. 9 Pool/Getty Images; p. 12 © iStockphoto.com/Kerstin Waurick; p. 13 Hero Images/Getty Images; p. 16 Jean-Christophe Verhaegen/AFP/Getty Images; p. 18 HomeArt/Shutterstock.com; p. 21 Becky Stern/beckystern.com; p. 22 LValeriy/Shutterstock.com; p. 25 tmc-photos/Shutterstock.com; p. 27 © iStockphoto.com/Susan Chiang; p. 29 Christian Jung/Shutterstock.com; p. 31 The Christian Science Monitor/Getty Images; p. 35 Dragon Images/Shutterstock.com; p. 37 Plusea/Flickr/https://www.flickr.com/photos/plusea/24706892049/CC BY 2.0; p. 39 Ozgur Guvenc/Shutterstock.com; p. 43 Architecteur/Shutterstock.com; p. 45 GH1 WENN Photos/Newscom; p. 48 Globe Newswire/AP Images; p. 50 Anna Hoychuk/Shutterstock.com; p. 52 Matthew Ashton/Corbis Sport/Getty Images; cover and interior pages background pattern Slanapotam/Shutterstock.com.

Designer: Nicole Russo; Editor: Bernadette Davis;
Photo Researcher: Nicole DiMella